RUTH GOODE

HANDS UP!

DRAWINGS BY
ANTHONY KRAMER

MACMILLAN PUBLISHING COMPANY
NEW YORK

COLLIER MACMILLAN PUBLISHERS
LONDON

Also by Ruth Goode

People of the Ice Age

People of the First Cities

A Book for Grandmothers

For Aviva and Jonathan
who inspired this
book

Macmillan Publishing Company
866 Third Avenue, New York, N.Y. 10022
Collier Macmillan Canada, Inc.

Printed in the United States of America
10 9 8 7 6 5 4 3 2 1

Library of Congress Cataloging in Publication Data

Goode, Ruth.
  Hands up!

  Bibliography: p.
  Summary: Describes the evolutionary development of the
hand, explains how hands work, and examines right- and
left-handedness, the myth of double-jointedness, motor
development, and hand-eye-brain coordination.
  1. Hand—Juvenile literature. [1. Hand] I. Kramer,
Anthony, ill. II. Title.
QM548.G66   611'.97   81-82018
ISBN 0-02-736550-6

CONTENTS

1 Only People Have Hands   1

2 How Did Hands Come to Be?   4

3 How Do Hands Work?   7

4 How It Bleeds!   11

5 How Do Hands Learn?   14

6 More About How Hands Work   18

7 What Are Fingerprints?   20

8 Right Hand, Left Hand   24

9 Hands Can Talk   26

10 Hands Can Tell Stories   30

11 Hands Can Play Games   34

12 Hands Can Make Pictures   42

13 Musical Hands and Puppet Fingers   48

14 Hands Can Do Magic   54

Further Reading   59

ONLY PEOPLE HAVE HANDS

Look around and you will see that most animals do not have hands. Birds have wings where their hands would be. Fish have fins. Most animals have four feet and they walk on all fours.

Cows and horses, goats and deer have hoofs. So do giraffes.

These are animals that live on plant foods. They eat grass and leaves, and the twigs and bark of trees. Animals with hoofs run and walk on the tips of their toes. A hoof is a special kind of toenail that grows very hard and tough. It grows big enough to cover the ends of the toes altogether, like a hard little shoe. Their hoofs help these animals to run fast over rough ground, to get away from the animals that hunt them.

Hunting animals have paws that go softly over the ground, almost without a sound. Their quiet paws are very useful in hunting. Cats and lions, dogs and wolves are hunting animals. Members of the cat family have toenails that are claws. They have special muscles in their paws to push their claws out for fighting or climbing.

Seals and whales have flippers that work like paddles when they swim. When you learn to swim, your swimming teacher tells you to keep your fingers together, so that they will work like a seal's flippers in the water.

On monkeys, all four feet are very much like hands, thumbs and all—very useful for swinging through the trees and picking the fruit that they eat. When they run on the ground they go on all four feet.

Some of the big apes—the chimpanzees and gorillas—walk on their two hind feet and the knuckles of their hands. Watch them do this, the next time you go to the zoo.

Look at all the animals, and you will see that only people have hands that are never used as feet, except to do acrobatic tricks. Only people have hands that they use just to hold and carry things and work with tools.

Our hands make us different from all other living creatures.

How Do the Animals Manage without Hands?

If the animals have no hands like ours, how do they do all the things they do?

They all have different ways.

Your dog holds down his bone with his paw while he chews at it. Your cat wets her forepaw with her tongue to wash her face, and then she washes herself everywhere else with her tongue. A mother cat washes her kittens all over with her tongue, until they learn to wash themselves.

Birds pick up things with their beaks. They carry straws and whatever they need up into the tree to make a nest, and they weave the nest with their beaks.

Birds that eat seeds crack the seeds in their beaks and spit out the shells. You can watch the house finches do that at your bird feeder.

The weaver finch holds a thorn in its beak the way you would hold a tool in your hand, and it uses the thorn the same way. It pokes out grubs and insects from the bark of a tree for its food.

A sea gull drops a clam on the rocks and then swoops down to peck the juicy clam out of its broken shell.

A California sea otter has an even trickier way of getting a shellfish out of its shell. The otter floats on its back with a flat stone on its chest and bangs the shellfish on the rock with its two forepaws until the shell breaks.

A squirrel sits up and cracks a nut with its strong teeth, holding the nut between its two forepaws.

A monkey can hold a banana in one hand. It is almost the only animal that can do that. But it could probably hold the banana just as well with its foot!

Monkeys can pick bugs and burrs out of their own and each other's coats with their fingertips. So can some apes. The baboons are apes that eat seeds, and they can pick up things as tiny as we can.

A chimpanzee is a very clever ape, but it can never pick up small objects with a thumb and forefinger. It has a long palm and a short thumb, too short to put thumb tip and fingertip together. If you gave a chimpanzee a grape, it would take the grape and hold it with its thumb against the side of its palm.

But if you gave a chimpanzee a piece of string you would never be able to take the string back, unless the chimpanzee wanted to give it to you. It would hold the string with its thumb against its palm, then fold its palm over that, and then curl its long fingers over that, making a fist with the thumb inside. The chimpanzee's double-lock grip is special for the way it gets its food. It can swing out on a thin branch or jungle vine and hang there by one hand without slipping, while it reaches for the young, tender leaves at the end of the branch.

2

HOW DID HANDS COME TO BE?

Our hands came to be the way they are a very long time ago. So did our feet. And so did all the special kinds of animal feet.

Before there were people in the world, there were many kinds of animals. Animals with hoofs ran on the ground, and animals with paws and claws hunted them. At that time, little animals like monkeys were living in trees.

Hoofs or paws would not be much use to monkeys in the trees. Instead, they had four fingers and a thumb on each of their four feet. With those, they could swing from branch to branch, using any of their four feet to reach and grab the next branch. They also had a tail that could curl around a branch, like a fifth hand to hold on with.

The big apes were like monkeys in many ways, but they were too big and heavy to live entirely in the trees. So they lived mostly on the ground. But they still walked on all fours, or on two feet and the knuckles of one hand. They could stand up to reach and climb and they could sit upright, but they could not walk or run on two feet.

Then came creatures that could stand and walk and run on two feet. They were the first human beings.

If you met some of those first human beings today, you would not think they were much like you or your friends. Their heads were small, and their faces were more like apes' faces than people's faces. Even when they were grown up they were no taller than someone eleven or twelve years old.

But they had feet like our feet and hands like our hands. They could carry things in their hands. They could pick up a stone or a stick and use it for hunting or fighting.

Hands Have Not Changed

Hands have not changed in millions of years. But people have changed. New people were born who were bigger, stronger,

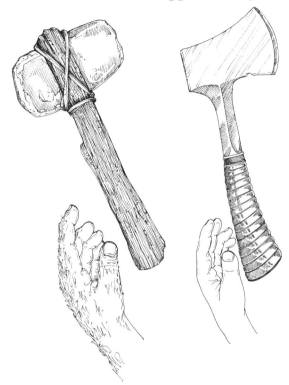

and smarter. They kept thinking of new things to do and make with their hands.

They made cutting and chopping tools out of stone. They made clothing. For a long time, people just wrapped an animal skin around themselves to keep warm, but that got in the way of using their arms and hands. So they figured out how to cut the animal skins into the shapes of shirts and coats with sleeves. They invented the needle—a piece of animal bone with a point at one end and a hole at the other—and stitched the clothing together with strips of animal skin.

We still make needles the same way, only we make them out of steel and we make them by machine. The people of long ago did not have metal, and they did not have machines. Their tools were of stone or bone, and they made everything by hand.

They made pots to cook in, out of clay that they baked in the fire. They made hatchets, spears, bows, and arrows. They carved designs and pictures of animals on their hunting weapons.

They mixed paints out of earth colors and made brushes out of animal hairs, and they painted pictures on the walls of their caves. They made flutes and drums out of animal bones and played music for dancing and singing.

Making New Things

Every time people thought of something new to make, their hands and brains had to work out the way to do it. Some of the things they made took a very long time to work out.

Most of the things we use today are made not by hand but by machines. Still, it was hands and brains, working together, that made the machines. Hands and brains made machines to make the paper we write on, the desks we sit at, the clothes we wear, the cars and trains and planes and spaceships we travel in.

All the things we have today are very different from the clay pots and stone axes and knives that people made long ago. But our hands are the same as theirs.

Hands have not changed, but only the things we have taught our hands to do.

A grown person's hands do a thousand different things in a single day. Probably your hands do almost as many.

3

HOW DO HANDS WORK?

Can you pat your head with one hand while you rub your stomach with the other? It makes you think hard about what each hand is doing!

Hands work separately in most of the things they do together. If you are hammering in a nail, one hand holds the nail while the other one swings the hammer. If you are making scrambled eggs, one hand holds the handle of the frying pan while the other one stirs the eggs.

When people do magic tricks, they say that the hand is quicker than the eye. But the real magic is getting the audience to watch the wrong hand. While the audience is watching one hand, the other hand is getting the trick ready. The next time you go to a magic show, try to watch the hand the magician doesn't want you to watch.

Fingers have to learn to work separately, too. When you learn to use a typewriter, each finger has certain letters to tap. When you play a musical instrument, each finger has its own notes to play. A very good musician playing a very fast piece plays hundreds of notes a minute, and he uses all his fingers to do it.

A baseball pitcher uses his fingers in different ways to throw the ball. He places his fingers on the ball one way to throw a curve, another way to throw a drop, still another way to throw a floater. The different way he places his fingers gives the ball a different spin. The spin makes the ball travel in different ways across home plate.

Most people don't have to do magic or play the piano or throw a curve ball. But everybody's hands learn to do many different kinds of things. Hands learn to pick up things as tiny as a seed or as big as a watermelon. Hands learn to write with a pencil or a pen. They learn to draw pictures and paint them with paints and brushes. They learn to turn a screw with a screwdriver and saw a board with a saw.

Hands learn to count out money. They learn to work the keys of a calculator, the dials of a radio, a television set, a computer.

Hands have to become strong. Your hand has to use one and one-quarter pounds of force to pick up a glass of water. It has to use two and one-half pounds to unscrew the top of a toothpaste tube, six and one-half pounds to turn a doorknob.

How do hands and fingers do all these different kinds of things? How do they actually *work*?

Fingers and Thumb

A hand looks simple. It has four fingers pointing forward and a thumb pointing to the side. The fingers are thicker or thin-

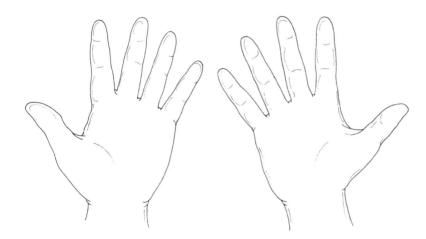

ner, longer or shorter. No two fingers are exactly the same size.

The thumb is short but it is the thickest and strongest. When you hold a hammer by its handle, watch what your thumb does. Your fingers go around one side of the handle, but your thumb goes around the opposite side. Your thumb locks over your fingers to make a strong grip.

When you use scissors, see how the thumb has one half of the handle to itself. The thumb moves one of the two blades of the scissors while the fingers move the other. If we did not have a thumb that works opposite to the fingers, there are many tools we could not use very well. And we could not use scissors at all!

Curl your fingers over and look at your knuckles. Knuckles are joints that work like hinges on a door. They bend your fingers to make a fist, and they straighten them to make an open hand.

Each finger can bend or straighten separately. But not every finger does this equally well. Your ring finger and your little finger are not as good at working alone as your forefinger and your middle finger.

Are You Double-Jointed?

Like the hinges on a door, your knuckles can bend only one way, toward your palm. Some people can bend their fingers so far back that we call them double-jointed. But they really do not have double joints. Their knuckles are hinge joints like everyone's. They are simply more rubbery. Children's fingers are usually more rubbery than grown-ups' fingers.

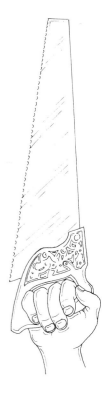

The wrist is another kind of joint. It can bend in all directions. The wrist bends most of all to the front, but it can bend back and to the sides quite a bit. It bends almost twice as far to the little finger side as to the thumb side, but when it bends to the thumb side it is twice as strong.

You find this out when you use tools. When you use a screwdriver, your wrist bends toward the little finger and gives you a longer turn of the screw. When you use a chisel, your wrist bends toward the thumb and you can dig deeper or scrape harder.

Your hand has twenty-seven bones, thirty joints, and thirty-two muscles. All together, that makes eighty-nine different parts. All the parts are tiny. But they are fitted and connected together to make your hand work, like a very fine machine.

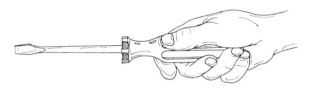

The Muscles Are the Motors

If a hand were a machine, the muscles would be its motors. When a muscle tightens, it pulls on the bones across a joint and bends the hinge. It takes seven or eight tiny muscles just to move one of your fingers. It takes ten muscles to move your thumb.

Strong cords connect the muscles to the bones and joints to make them move. These cords are called tendons and ligaments. In some places these cords have to go over or under other parts of the hand to connect with the part they must move. They have little tunnels to go through, so that they can do their job and not get tangled with other parts.

When you sprain a finger or a thumb, it is these cords that usually get stretched and hurt. The doctor ties up the sprain to rest the hurt parts so that they can heal. If it is a bad sprain or if a bone has cracked, the doctor may put the whole hand in a cast. That way, the bone can heal its crack, and the injured muscles and cords can rest and get well.

4

HOW IT BLEEDS!

Did you ever wonder why your finger bleeds so much when you cut it?

A finger bleeds so much because hands and fingers have a very rich supply of blood vessels. Hands and fingers need all these blood vessels in order to do the many things they have to do.

The blood vessels are like two sets of little pipes or tubes. One set is to bring and the other set is to carry away.

The tubes coming into the hand bring blood carrying oxygen and foods of many kinds to keep the bones and muscles healthy and working. These blood vessels that bring in the supplies are called arteries.

The arteries bring this good supply of blood from the heart. They are quite thick little tubes as they come down inside the shoulder and the arm into the wrist. Then they branch off inside the hand into thinner and thinner tubes, as thin as fine threads. They carry the blood supply into every muscle and bone and right to the tips of the fingers.

There is a whole network of tiny blood vessels spreading inside each fingertip. They bring a lot of nourishing blood into the fingertips.

From the fingertips, the tiny tubes begin to come together again into larger tubes. These carry away the blood that has delivered foods and picked up the used materials that the hand no longer needs.

The tubes that carry the used blood away are called veins. You can say that the arteries and veins together are like a grocery delivery and garbage collection system, all in one.

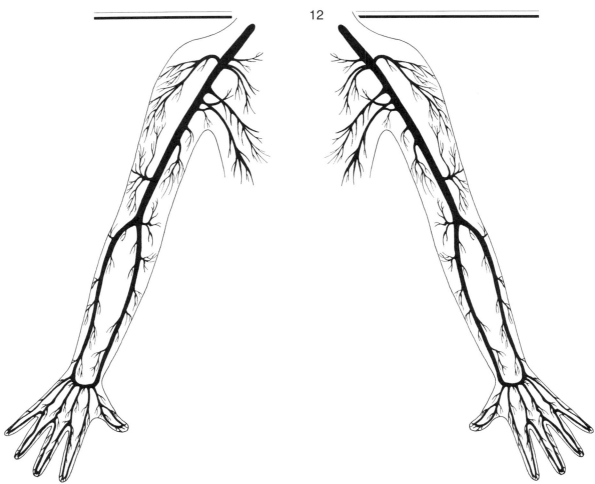

If you look at your wrist, you may see the veins there. Under the thin skin on the underside of your wrist, the veins look rather blue. Blood is bright red when it is carrying oxygen, but after it delivers its oxygen it becomes quite dark. So the blood in the veins is dark red, and through the skin it looks blue.

You can't see the arteries from the outside. They are safely placed deep inside the wrist. But if you put your finger on your wrist, about halfway between the middle and the little finger side, you can feel something moving there. It feels like a tiny drum beating.

That is the blood moving along the artery into your hand. The little beating movement is your pulse. When you go to the doctor, he puts his finger on your pulse and counts its beats. Your pulse is one of the ways that your body tells him how well and strong it is.

When you have been running, or you are hot or excited, your pulse speeds up. When you sit still for a while, it quiets down to its normal rate.

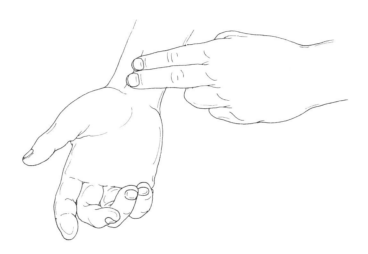

Generally speaking, small bodies have a faster pulse than large ones, and that is true for babies and little kids. But by the time boys and girls are ten, eleven, or twelve years old their pulse rate has settled down to what is normal for grown-ups, between seventy and eighty beats per minute. You can take your own pulse, or your friend's, by putting your finger on the little beat and counting while the second hand on your clock or watch makes one complete revolution, marking the passage of a minute. Any finger will do for taking a pulse—except your thumb, because the thumb has a pulse of its own, very faint but just enough to mix things up.

5

HOW DO HANDS LEARN?

Why can your hands do so many things a baby's hands can't do? A baby can barely pick up a spoon without dumping the contents. But you can use a knife and fork, paint a picture, write your name. How do hands learn?

Hands learn because they get messages from the brain telling them what to do. The messengers are the nerves.

The nerves are the other important network. Like the blood vessels, the nerves spread everywhere into the hand and the fingers. They are like the very thinnest threads. Think of them as wires, linked together like a very special telephone system carrying messages to and from the brain. The messages are sent without a sound, by a kind of tiny electric spark along the nerve wires.

Let's see how the nerves take their messages. Would you like to pick up your pencil? Your brain sends the message along the nerves to the muscles in your arm and hand and fingers, to move to the pencil and pick it up. Then the nerves send the message back to your brain that you are holding the pencil in your fingers.

The next message from the brain tells your muscles what you want to write, and they do it.

It's a lucky thing that you don't have to tell each tiny muscle just how to move to do its job, or you would never get anything written at all! Your brain and the nerves have already learned the way without your having to tell them.

Do you remember how it was when you were learning to write? It was hard work, and you had to practice and practice. When we practice doing a particular thing, the nerves learn to

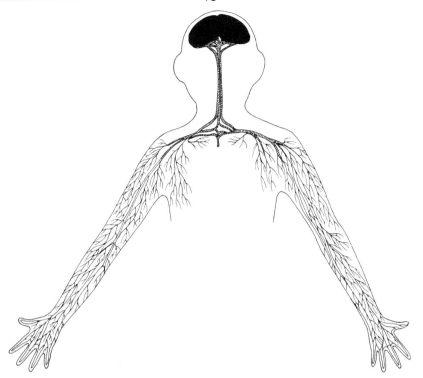

carry the messages along the pathways to the particular muscles, and the muscles learn to work together to do what we
want them to do. Most of the things we do with our hands need
many muscles working smoothly together.

Practice does indeed make perfect. Practice makes the nerve
messages go smoothly along the right pathways to the right
muscles, and they do what we want them to do without our
having to think about them.

Messages That Go the Other Way

The nerves that carry messages from the brain to the muscles
are called the motor nerves. A motor makes things move.

Messages go the other way, too. They go from hands and
fingers to the brain. These messages go along different nerves.

They are called the sensory nerves, meaning that they tell us how things feel.

The sensory nerves are of different kinds, to carry different messages. If you put your finger under the cold water tap, the nerves for cold tell you that the water is cold and how cold it is. If you put it under the hot water tap, the nerves that feel heat tell you that the water is warm or hot.

Close your eyes and touch things around you. Touch the page of this book, the edge of the page, the cover of the book. Touch the table, your shirt, your pants or skirt, your ear, your hair. Without looking, you know what you are touching. The message from your fingers tells you how each thing feels—whether it is rough or smooth, hard or soft, sharp or round.

There are more sensory nerves in your fingertips than anywhere else in your body, except your tongue.

Little babies are forever putting things in their mouths. Why do they do that? They do it to find out how things feel. They feel things better with their tongues than with their fingertips. As they grow older they will not need to use their tongues. The messages from their fingertips will tell them what they want to know.

Here is a trick you can try on yourself. Pick up your pencil with one hand. Now cross the forefinger and the middle finger of your other hand. And now, shut your eyes and rub the pencil gently between the two fingers, just above the place where they are crossed.

How many pencils do you feel? One pencil? Two pencils? You know it is only one pencil, but it certainly feels like two! Why is that?

Probably you can figure out the answer. It's because the nerves the pencil is touching are on the outer sides of those fingers. If the fingers were not crossed, it would take two pencils to touch those nerves, one against each finger. So the

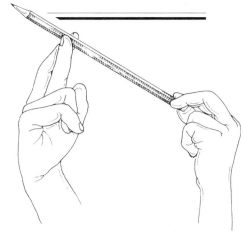

message goes back to your brain that there are two pencils.

That gives you an idea of the way those nerves are exactly placed to send the right messages to your brain, unless you play a trick on them and cross your fingers.

Try the trick on a friend. But be sure to have your friend close his or her eyes before you pick up the one pencil. Then he or she will be absolutely certain that you are touching those crossed fingers with two!

6

MORE ABOUT HOW HANDS WORK

Here is another set of nerves to test. Close your eyes again and move your hand. Put it up in the air. Put it on your head. Put it on your knee. Open your fingers and spread them wide. Close them and make a fist. Put one finger out straight, then another. Touch a finger to your nose.

Even with your eyes shut tight, you know exactly where your hand is, and what each finger is doing.

That is a very clever set of nerves. They are called the proprioceptive nerves, pronounced *pro-pre-o-sep-tive*. It is a word that means feeling the movements of parts of your own body. Every part of the body has these self-feeling nerves.

There is still another set of self-feeling nerves—the nerves for pain. Fingers are very well supplied with these pain nerves. That is why they hurt so much when we injure them.

Pain is a most important message. It tells you that you have hurt yourself, and it tells you just where you are hurt. It is a warning message, telling you that you must take care of the hurt part so that it can rest and heal itself.

The pain nerves tell you: *Look out now, take care of this, this hurt place needs help to get well.*

Too Hot to Touch!

There is another self-feeling message that comes to your brain, and it is a very special one because it comes so fast.

Suppose you touch something that is hot enough to burn you.

Have you ever done that? Have you noticed how your hand jumps away all by itself, even before you know that the thing is too hot to touch?

Did you ever get hold of a hot pot handle and then drop the pot and spill everything on the floor? Then you know how fast your hand lets go! And even so, you may have burned your fingers.

The too-hot message is so fast because it doesn't go all the way to the brain. It goes to a halfway station in the spinal cord, a cord of many nerves that is protected inside the bones of the backbone—the spine.

The too-hot message goes to the halfway station and the answer comes back in much less than a second: *Drop it!*

There are other messages that go to halfway stations. They are called reflexes. This particular one is called the "hot stove reflex," because that's just what it is. These very fast reflex messages are ways that the nervous system protects us from getting hurt.

7

WHAT ARE FINGERPRINTS?

When you rub your fingertips together they feel quite smooth. But look at them closely. You will see that they are really not smooth at all. Each fingertip has hundreds of tiny lines. The lines go in curves and circles, swirls and whorls.

No one else in the world has the same fingertip lines that you have. No two people have the same fingerprints. Even twins do not have exactly the same fingerprints.

If you have an ink pad for printing designs or letters of the alphabet, you can make your fingerprints. Press your fingertips, one by one, first on the ink pad, then on a clean sheet of paper. Those are your fingerprints. Can you see the whorls and swirls?

Get a friend to make fingerprints, too. Can you see that they are not the same as yours?

Palms Are Different, Too

Not only your fingerprints are special to you. Look at the inside of your hand—the part that we call the palm. Do you see the lines there? Now look at your friend's palm and yours, side by side. The lines come in about the same places, but they are not exactly the same.

And here is something even more peculiar. Your own two palms are not exactly the same as each other! As you get older, the lines in one hand will keep getting even more different from those on the other.

This happens because the lines come where the hands fold to grasp something or to make a fist. Your hand is full of many small muscles. The palm of your hand also has soft places, like

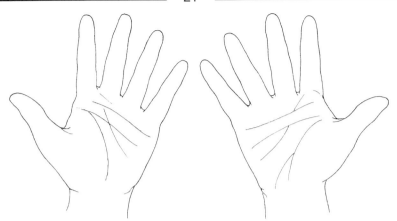

little pillows. These are tiny cushions of fat that protect the joints and the bones.

Suppose you are hammering something. Think how it would hurt the little bones in your hand every time you bang the hammer down. That's why your hand needs its little pillows.

The lines in your palm form along the muscles and around the little pillows. There are very many little muscles and connections in a hand, and no two hands are exactly alike.

Your own two hands are not alike, because you use your two hands to do different things. One hand holds your book and the other turns the page. One hand holds your paper and the other writes on it. One hand holds the nail and the other swings the hammer.

You may use both hands together for some jobs—to carry a heavy box or turn a stiff handle. But most of the time the hands help each other by doing different parts of the job. And in that way, different muscles become bigger and stronger, and they make little changes in the lines of the palm.

The Tough, Smooth Skin

The skin of our hands is exactly suited to what hands have to do. On the back the skin is smooth and fine. On some people, usually grown men, it is often hairy. It is like the skin on arms and legs and chests.

But the skin on the palm is thick and tough and, except for the lines, it is very smooth.

The tiny lines on the fingertips help to keep things from slipping when we pick them up. The palm does not have those hundreds of tiny lines. It has something else.

All over the palm are many little sweat glands. They are too tiny for you to see. They are like tiny faucets. When a person is doing hard work, like chopping wood, the tiny faucets open and the palm becomes damp. When it is damp, the skin gets a stronger grip on the handle of the axe than when it is dry.

Have you ever noticed that when a man takes up a tool he may spit on his hands first? He knows from experience that moist palms give him a firm grip.

People say, "I'm going to spit on my hands and get the job done." They say that even when the job has nothing to do with swinging a heavy tool. It's a way of saying that they are really going to get to work.

Fingernails

Fingernails are a useful part of hands. They protect the ends of fingers, and they help pick up things that are very small or very thin, like pins or needles.

Fingernails are harder than skin but not as hard as bone, and they keep growing and having to be trimmed, like hair. Milk is one of the foods that help make fingernails strong. It helps make bones strong, too. Milk and foods made with milk, like cheese, contain calcium. Fingernails and bones need calcium to make them hard and firm.

Did you ever jam your finger so hard that the fingernail turned dark? Then the dark part grew out, and the new part growing in was nice and pink again. Sometimes a nail is hurt so badly that it falls off. But in a few weeks a new nail grows in its place. Where does it grow from?

Down in the finger, below the edge of the skin that we call the cuticle, is a growing place for the nail called the nail bed. As long as the nail bed is not hurt, it will keep growing a new nail. If the nail bed is a little hurt it may grow a new nail with a dent or a wrinkle in it. But as time goes by, the nail bed usually gets well again and can grow a smooth nail.

8

RIGHT HAND, LEFT HAND

Most people write and cut and do most one-handed jobs with their right hands. About one person out of every eight or nine uses the left hand instead.

More boys than girls are left-handed, and left-handedness usually runs in the family.

There is nothing wrong with being left-handed. It is just different.

It is also very often inconvenient, because so many things are designed for the seven out of eight—or eight out of nine—people who are right-handed. If you are left-handed, or you have a friend who is, think of some things that are made for right-handed people that are hard or even impossible for a left-handed person to use. Can openers, for instance.

The difference between right-handedness and left-handedness begins in the way the brain is arranged. Have you ever seen a picture of the brain? It looks like a walnut and, like a walnut without its shell, the brain is divided down the middle into two halves.

Each half has different jobs. The left half of the brain directs the right side of the body, and the right half directs the left side. There is a place far down in the back of the brain where the nerves for each side of the body cross over.

A baby at first doesn't seem to use one hand more than the other. It will reach for a spoon or a toy with either hand. But as the baby grows, one side of the brain becomes stronger. By the time the baby is a toddler, it is usually either a right-handed or a left-handed person.

In most people the left side of the brain becomes stronger,

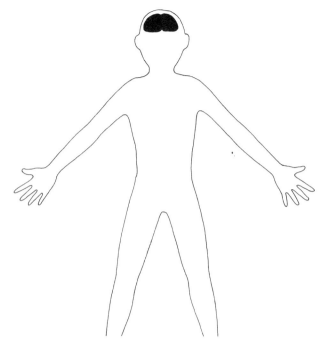

and so the baby becomes right-handed. But if a child seems to prefer its left hand, it just means that in that little boy or girl the right side of the brain is getting to be the stronger side.

People used to believe they had to force a child who turned out to be left-handed to use its right hand. But now parents and teachers don't fuss over whether a child uses the right hand or the left.

A very few people seem to use both hands equally well. For them it seems that neither side of the brain has become stronger than the other. Sometimes a person is "both-handed" because he or she was really left-handed to begin with and was taught to use the right hand. When a person has a badly injured hand or arm, he or she may have to learn to use the other hand. The word for people who use both hands equally well is "ambidextrous."

9

HANDS CAN TALK

When you have a little accident, like knocking over a glass of milk, what do you say? "Oh, my!" is what most people say, or something that means the same thing.

Have you ever noticed what your hands do? They say, "Oh, my!" too. They say it by going to your mouth. Or to the sides of your head. Or just up in the air.

Every time we talk, our hands talk, too. Often our hands talk when we don't make a sound.

Think of all the different times that your hands talk for you. In school, when the teacher asks a question and you know the answer, do you put your hand up in the air? Do you wave it around to attract the teacher's attention? Does your hand try to say that you want to be the one to give the answer?

Suppose your teacher asks you a question, and you don't know the answer. How does your hand say you don't know, or you're not sure?

A baby puts a finger in its mouth when it is not sure or feels mixed up. Older children and grown-ups usually don't put fingers in their mouths, but they may put a finger to their lips. Our hands have different ways of saying we don't know. The way our hands say this may also show that we are upset at not knowing. Or our hands may say that we don't know and don't care!

How would your hands say that?

Everybody Knows These Hand Words

There are many hand words that everybody knows. People say, "Come here" or "Go there." They say, "I want this" or "I don't

want that." They put up one, two, or three fingers to say how many of something.

They make a circle with the thumb and forefinger to say "Okay!" They point a thumb down to say "No way!"

They point a thumb along the road to say they want a lift. They point a finger to say "You go that way" or "Look at that!"

The traffic policeman puts his hand up with the palm out to say "Stop!" He waves his hand across himself to say "Go ahead."

Hands Tell Our Feelings

Hands tell our feelings in many different ways. Usually we understand what they are telling us. When a grown-up shakes a forefinger at you, you know very well that that grown-up is cross with you. "Don't you ever do that again!" that finger is saying.

When someone makes a fist and shakes it in the air, you know he is angry. When you see someone clap her hands together you know she is happy and perhaps also surprised.

When a person puts a hand over her mouth it may tell you

she is frightened or upset. When your friend puts out a hand for you to shake, especially after you have had a quarrel, you know that that means "Let's be friends again."

People in different countries have different ways of saying good-by. We wave a hand away from us. Italian people wave a hand with the fingers toward themselves. That says good-by, but it also says "See you again!"

We all have different ways of saying hello, too. Some people shake hands for both hello and good-by. Some put their other hand on the friend's shoulder, or they clasp it over the two clasped hands. That says that they have very warm feelings for their friend—happy feelings at meeting and sad feelings at parting.

In some countries a person greets another person by putting his two hands together and then bowing over them. Another greeting is to touch a finger to the forehead, the lips, and the heart, and then to put the hands together and bow. That is a way of saying "My thoughts, my words, and my feelings are all for you."

Shaking hands to show friendship is a very old custom. It began long ago, when people did not usually trust strangers. If the stranger meant no harm, he would put out his right hand to show that there was no sword or dagger in it. The other man would do the same. Then they would clasp hands as a way of sealing the friendship.

People use their hands in different ways to pray. Putting the two hands together with the palms facing each other is the way most people pray in the Western countries. Sometimes a person will put his hands over his eyes, to pray silently.

Hands Talk Around the World

People all over the world talk to each other with their hands. Even when they don't know each other's language, their hands

can still talk. Hands have their own language. Try telling your friend something, without saying a word, and you'll see. Your hands will find ways of saying what you want to say.

Long ago in America the Indians belonged to different tribes, and the tribes had different languages. The Indians still belong to different tribes. But now they talk to each other in English.

In the old days, when they had no language that they all could speak, they had a whole sign language that they talked with their hands.

The deaf language is a whole language that people talk with their hands. Do you know the letters of the deaf alphabet? Some of the signs say a whole word at once. Some can say a whole sentence. When someone we know is deaf, we can learn to talk with the person with our hands.

HANDS CAN TELL STORIES

In India, Hawaii, and some other places, dancers tell long stories without saying or singing a word, but just by using their hands.

Your hands can tell whole stories, too.

When children are little, their first stories are hand stories. "This little piggy went to market" is the first story grown-ups tell to babies, and it is a finger story.

Many of the Mother Goose stories are hand as well as word stories. Here is one:

> *Hickory dickory dock*
>   (hang your hand down and swing it back and forth like the pendulum of a clock)
> *The mouse ran up the clock*
>   (put your hands together side by side and wriggle your thumbs and pinky fingers underneath for the mouse)
> *The clock struck one*
>   (clap your hands sharply once)
> *The mouse ran down*
>   (make the mouse run down)
> *Hickory dickory dock*
>   (swing your hand for the pendulum again)

"Rockabye, baby, in the treetop" is another easy hand-and-word story. For "rockabye," link your fingers with the palms up and cup them to make the cradle. One thumb lying inside the palm makes the baby.

For "treetop," put your elbows and wrists together to make the tree trunk with your arms, and spread your hands at the top to make the leaves. For "When the wind blows," make your

Hickory dickory dock

The mouse ran up the clock

The clock struck one

The mouse ran down

Hickory dickory dock

tree sway from side to side, farther and farther over, and "The cradle will rock."

Then, "Down comes the cradle, baby and all." And down it comes, with the baby (your thumb) in the cradle, sitting up and looking over the edge.

"Here is a church" is a hand story most children know. For the church, link your fingers closely together and turn your palms to face each other, with the fingers inside and the thumbs together at the front.

For "Here is the steeple," put your two forefingers up with the tips meeting in a point.

"Open the door" and spread your thumbs apart like a double door opening.

"And here are the people"—turn hands over, and your fingers, wriggling inside, are the people!

Make Up Your Own Hand Stories

You can make up your own hand stories. Here are some hand and finger signs that you can use:

Make a bird flying by linking your thumbs together and flapping your hands to the sides for the wings.

Make a bird sitting in a tree by making a fist with your thumb sticking up and slightly bent for the bird's head. Make the bird put its head under its wing and go to sleep by tucking your thumb inside your fist.

Make the bird sitting on its eggs in the nest. The nest is one hand, palm up and fingers curled. The bird is the other hand in a fist sitting on top, with the forefinger up and slightly curled for the bird's neck and head.

Make a fish swimming by putting one hand on top of the other with the palms down, fingers together, and the thumbs at each side sticking out and moving to make the fins. Lift the top middle finger a tiny bit and put it down again to make the fish open and close its mouth while swimming.

Two hands folded together into a cup are a bird's nest. The fingers inside are the little birds.

Your fist can be a house, with the thumb for a door that opens and closes. Your two hands with the fingers folded flat over each other at the top make a window.

Your fist can be a box. Tuck the thumb inside the fist and then pop it up suddenly, and that's a jack-in-the-box.

A fist with an open top is a beehive. The fingers of the other hand are the bees flying in and out. Open the fist and turn it with the palm up and the fingers curled like petals, and you have a flower to which the bees come to take pollen and nectar for their honey.

Rest your fingertips and your elbow on the table and lift up your wrist, and there's a hill. Move your hand with the fingers together in winding curves along the table and that's a river or a road. Link the fingers of your two hands together out flat, and put your thumbs straight down with the tips resting on the table, and that's a bridge.

Walk your forefinger and middle finger along the table, with the other fingers and the thumb curled up, and that's a person walking. Walk the forefinger and pinky finger of one hand behind the forefinger and pinky finger of the other, and that's a horse or a cow. (The four-legged animals take a little practice.)

You can invent your own hand and finger signs to make your story all the more fun to tell and to listen to.

11
HANDS CAN PLAY GAMES

Here is a game of matching strength that you can play with a friend.

Put your elbows out at your sides and your hands flat against your chest. Keep your wrists straight. Let the tips of your middle fingers just touch each other.

Now ask your friend to take hold of your wrists and try to pull your hands apart.

If you hold tight against his pull, he will probably not be able to pull your hands apart.

Are you really stronger than your friend?

Try it the other way around. Let your friend hold his hands the way you did. Now you try to pull his hands apart.

Can you do it? Probably not. Probably you are both about equally strong.

A game of strength that grown-ups like to play is hand wrestling. Try it with a friend.

Each of you rests the right elbow on the table, touching one to the other. Then you put your forearms up against each other. Then each takes hold of the other's hand with a strong grip.

Now try to push your friend's hand down on the table. Meanwhile, your friend tries to push your hand down on the table.

Whoever gets the other's hand down first wins the wrestling match.

Hands Learn by Playing Games

Children all over the world play hand and finger games. So do grown-ups. When there is a baby in the family, the grown-ups and the older brothers and sisters play hand games with the baby.

The hand games are fun for the baby—and for the brothers and sisters, too. Games are also one of the best ways that hands and fingers learn.

You surely don't remember the first hand games you played with an older person when you were a baby. Your hands learned lots of other things when you were a baby and a toddler. Probably you can't remember learning any of them.

Can you remember the first time you were able to hold a spoon right side up and get the cereal to your mouth? When you first put the sugar on your cereal without spilling? When you first poured your own glass of milk or juice? When you first broke your egg into your cup without dropping in the shell? Or dropping the egg on the floor?

It takes a long time to manage a spoon. It takes even longer to manage a fork and then a knife. Chinese and Japanese children have to learn to eat with chopsticks. Can you eat with chopsticks?

These are not games. But games help hands and fingers to learn how to manage eating tools, working tools, and many other things.

Hardly anybody can remember learning these first things. So don't be surprised that you can't remember when you first learned to play Pat-a-Cake with one of your parents or grandparents, or with your big brother or sister.

Pat-a-Cake is a hard game for babies to learn. Just clapping hands is harder for a baby than you would think.

The first game babies learn is usually the much easier one of Peek-a-Boo. First you do it for the baby. Hide your face behind your hands and then peek out suddenly and say "Boo!" Most babies laugh at that. Then the baby will try to do the same.

Clap Hands comes next. Then comes Pat-a-Cake. At first, all the baby can do is hold up its hands for the older person to clap. Then the baby learns to clap its hands together. And then it can clap its hands to the other person's hands. The last thing the baby learns is crossing its hands over to clap the other person's opposite hand.

A game played just about everywhere is Matching Fingers. You match fingers when you choose up sides to play softball or some other team game.

Do you know the game? You hold your hands behind your back. Then you call out "Odd!" or "Even!" At the same moment, you quickly put out your hands with several fingers sticking out of your fist. You may choose to put out as many fingers as you like or none at all—just your fist. Your friend does the same.

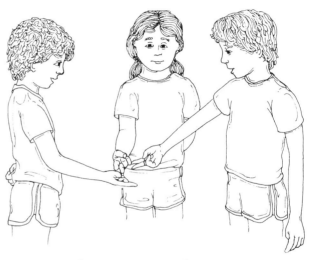

Then you count all the fingers together, yours and your friend's, to see if they add up to an odd number or an even number. If you made the right call, you win.

String Games Around the World

Do you know the game of Cat's Cradle?

It is only one of the many string games that children and grown-ups play everywhere in the world.

Indian children in the jungle of South America play Cat's Cradle. So do children in Korea and Japan, and in England and France.

Grown-ups play Cat's Cradle, too. They play many other string games.

They make pictures with the string, holding it in different ways on their hands. They make a picture of a palm tree, a fish in a pond, a moth, a man on a bed.

American Indians make a string picture of an Indian house or tent. Eskimos make the same picture for an Eskimo house, an igloo. In the Eskimo game, the house falls down and two boys run away from it. The whole story is told with a piece of string on the person's two hands.

Cat's Cradle is the string game that most people know best. Nobody really knows how it came to be called Cat's Cradle.

The game is played by two people. Each time one player takes the string from the other player, he makes it into a different figure by the way he takes it.

If a player makes a mistake in the way he takes the string from the other player's fingers, he ends up with a snarl instead of a figure. Then the players have to begin from the beginning again.

You need a length of string, about as long as you are tall and a little more. Take the two ends and tie a square knot.

Tying the Knot

Do you know how to tie a square knot? Tying knots of all kinds is one of the important things that fingers learn to do.

To tie a square knot, hold the two ends of the string, one in each hand. Put the right-hand end over the left-hand end, and then under it. Now you are holding the two ends in the opposite hands.

Put the left-hand end over and under the right-hand end. This time it goes above the first half of the knot that you have already made.

You now have two small loops opposite each other. Pull both ends, and there's your square knot.

You can test whether it is really a square knot by pulling

one end out straight. You will be able to slide the knot off, and the knot will undo itself.

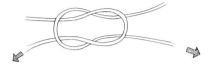

Playing Cat's Cradle

With the two ends of your string knotted together, you have a circle of string. You are ready to begin.

Put your hands in the circle of string and pull it straight in front of you. You have a loop over the back of each hand, with all your fingers inside except the thumbs.

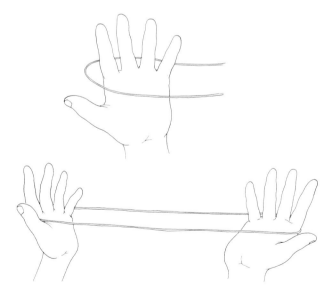

Now take another loop around each hand. You now have two strands of string across the back of each hand and one strand across each palm.

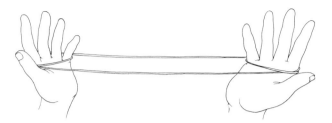

Put the middle finger of your right hand into the loop across your left palm and pull it across.

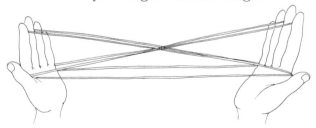

Put the middle finger of your left hand into the loop across your right palm—from underneath—and pull that across. The loop you pulled out on your left middle finger should be inside the loop you made with your right middle finger.

If you have done it right, that's the Cat's Cradle.

Now your partner will make the second figure. He takes hold of the strands of the two loops where they cross each other on each side. He holds each pair of strands with the forefinger and middle finger of each hand.

Then he moves his hands out to the sides, under the bottom

strands of the cradle, and up through the middle. He lifts the string off your fingers and spreads his hands apart.

If he has done it right, he has the second figure. People in different countries have different names for this figure. French people call it the scissors. English people call it a church window. Korean people call it a chess board.

To some people it is a soldier's bed, and to some others it is a fish pond. The Japanese have the most unusual name for it. They call it a house cat becoming a mountain cat.

Now it's your turn again. Take two crossing strands with the two fingers of each hand. Pull them out and under, and lift the string from your partner's hands onto your own. That's the third figure.

The English name for this figure is diamonds. The Koreans call it the cow's eyeball. The Japanese call it the horse eye. Americans say it is a cat's eye.

Some very skillful players go on to make a fourth figure, called a fish in a dish. But most of us take the third figure off in this way:

Hook the little finger of each hand into the outside strand on the opposite side of the figure. Do it like this: First, let the right-hand finger take the left side strand and then reach into that loop to let the left-hand finger take the right side strand. Now, with the thumb and forefinger of each hand, go underneath and into the diamonds at each end and lift the string from your partner's hands.

If you have done it right, you now have the original Cat's Cradle back again, but upside down!

So now begin again. If you work upside down with each figure, you may end up with your Cat's Cradle once more, right side up.

If it happens to be a long, rainy day, you may go round and round with your Cat's Cradles all day long!

12

HANDS CAN MAKE PICTURES

Hands can make pictures on the wall. You can give a whole picture show for your friends, just with your hands.

The pictures on the wall are shadow pictures. They are fun to do on dark winter afternoons. They are fun to do on any evening, any time of the year.

All you need to do is turn out all the lights in the room except one. That one light should shine on a plain wall. The best kind of lamp for this is a desk lamp that you can turn to shine on the wall.

Test your light. Put your hand in front of the light. Spread it out and wriggle your fingers.

Do you get a clear shadow on the wall? Can you see the shadow of your hand and each of your fingers? Then you are ready to begin.

Remember always to make your hand pictures in front of the light, so that the clear shadow picture falls on the wall.

You can make all kinds of animal pictures. Some pictures are made with one hand, some with both.

You can make a bird flying, a rabbit sitting, a goat with its beard, an elephant with its trunk.

You can make two giraffes feeding. You can make two people sitting on the grass.

How can you make all these pictures? You can make them just with your hands.

Shadow Birds

There is one picture you already know. That is the bird flying.

To make a picture of a bird flying, turn your hands with the palms facing you. Now cross your wrists, hook your two thumbs together, and spread your hands to the sides.

Your thumbs linked together make the bird's head and neck. Your hands spread to the sides are its wings.

Flap your hands. The bird is flying.

If you keep the fingers of each hand together so that no light shines between them, you have a picture of a pigeon or any small bird.

Now spread the fingers of each hand a little apart. That's a picture of a hawk. Those big hunting birds fly with the tips of their wing feathers spread just a little, so that the light shines between them.

To make an eagle, hold your hands back to back. Now link your little fingers. Make the top joint of one of your little fingers poke out above the other. That is the eagle's head and its sharp beak.

Now bend your wrists toward you, and bend your other fingers, close together, away from your linked little fingers. Those are the eagle's wings.

If your joints are quite rubbery, you may be able to flap the eagle's wings and set him flying, with his wing feathers spread a little bit apart like the hawk's.

Shadow Animals

You can make a rabbit with one hand. Fold your little finger and your ring finger down together and put your thumb over them. That's the rabbit's face.

Point your forefinger and middle finger up, one a little behind the other. Those are the rabbit's ears.

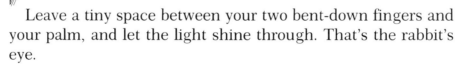

Leave a tiny space between your two bent-down fingers and your palm, and let the light shine through. That's the rabbit's eye.

To make the rest of the rabbit sitting up, you need your other hand. Put your other hand behind the first one, just above the wrist. Now let the tips of two fingers stick out. Those are its two short front legs dangling down in front of its body.

So now you have a whole rabbit, sitting up on its hind legs.

Two hands together, one on top of the other, can make a whole farmyard of animals one by one. They can make a whole zoo.

Stretch the fingers of your two hands out straight, and that's a horse with its long nose.

Bend them down a little for a dog, which has a shorter nose.

Bend them down still more for a bulldog, which has a flat face.

Let the tips of your thumbs stick up a little bit above the upper hand. Those are the animal's ears.

Make a pig with three fingers for its thick snout. Let the thumb stick forward underneath for its open mouth. The fleshy part of your hand below that thumb makes piggy's plump jaw. Let your other thumb stick up above the head of the pig for its ear. Leave a narrow slit between the top hand and the bottom hand for piggy's little slanty eye.

Make a deer with two fingers of the top hand sticking up for its horns.

Make a goat the same way, but bend your fingers a little for a goat's shorter nose. Tip the horns a bit forward. Let the little finger of the lower hand dangle down in a curve for the billy goat's beard.

Elephant and Camel

Make a picture of an elephant this way:

Bend your left hand down from the wrist and point the middle and ring fingers straight down together. That's the elephant's trunk.

Point the forefinger and little finger of that hand straight forward. Those are the elephant's tusks.

Let the thumb of that hand point forward under the trunk, leaving a little space between. That's the elephant's mouth, a little bit open.

Now put your right hand on top. Keep the knuckles of your right hand high enough to make the elephant's forehead and the top of its head. Bend the fingers down partway over the fingers of your left hand, just above the tusks. Leave a tiny space between your two hands for the elephant's eye.

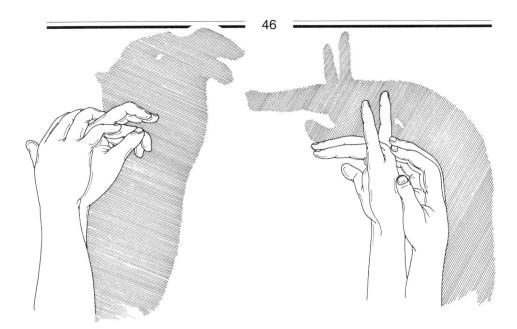

You may have to practice to get the trunk long enough and the forehead high enough. But once you get it right, it makes a very good shadow picture of an elephant.

Make a camel with one hand, like this:

Hold your left hand up with three fingers bent just a little. Let the little finger of that hand curl down. That's the camel's open mouth.

Let the tip of the thumb stick up at the top. That's the camel's ear.

Hold your whole arm in front of the light, with the elbow bent. That's the camel's long neck!

Swan and Goose

Your whole arm bent up from the elbow makes a swan's long neck.

Now, for the head—bend your hand forward at the wrist. Point your forefinger and thumb straight forward and a little bit apart for the swan's open beak. Bend the other three fin-

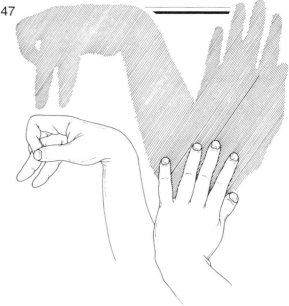

gers over your forefinger for the top of the head. Leave that little tiny space for the swan's eye.

Now for a special touch to the swan. Put your other hand against your arm, just above your bent elbow. Spread the fingers behind the swan's neck.

Now you have the whole swan, with the feathers of its wings!

You can turn the swan into a goose, just by bending the top fingers a little less to make a flatter head.

You can turn the goose into a duck by making a rounder top to its head, a shorter beak, and a short neck.

Part of the fun of shadow pictures is trying out new ones that you make up for yourself.

13

MUSICAL HANDS
AND PUPPET FINGERS

Hands can make music, even without instruments.

In many countries, clapping hands is part of the music. The clapping keeps time, especially for singing and dancing. The dancers make different sounds with their clapping, just by the way they hold their hands.

Try these different ways of clapping and you will hear the different sounds.

Clap your hands with the palms flat against each other. That is a high, flat sound.

Clap them with one hand a little lower than the other. That is a higher and flatter sound.

Clap the fingers of one hand against the palm of the other. That is a still higher, still flatter sound.

Now cup your palms and clap them together. That's a bigger, deeper sound. It is probably the loudest clapping sound your hands can make.

In faraway Eastern countries, people have a way of clapping the fingers of one hand against the palm of the other, changing hands each time and doing it very fast. It makes a special sound, and it beats time in a special way for their dancing.

Finger Music

People also make music with their fingers. In India the dancers sometimes wear little metal pieces on their fingertips. They clap them together to make sounds like little bells tinkling.

Spanish dancers make their finger music with little wooden clappers called castanets. They hold a pair of clappers in each hand. When they dance they clap them to make a sharp click-ing sound, keeping time with their steps.

For some dances they use just their snapping fingers. Span-ish dancers practice snapping their fingers to make a good loud sound. Their fingers become so strong that you can hear their sharp *snap snap snap* everywhere in the theater, no matter how far from the stage you are sitting.

Can you snap your fingers? If you practice, you will soon be able to do it.

Blowing Finger Music

Can you whistle?

Some people make a wonderful shrill whistle with their fin-gers.

Here is how:

Put your tongue against your lower teeth. Put the tips of your forefinger and middle finger into your mouth, between your teeth. Close your lips around your fingers, leaving a small space between them.

Now blow.

You will have to practice this quite a lot before you get a sound. Many people never learn how to do it.

If you know someone who can finger-whistle, ask him or her to show you how.

You can make a musical instrument with a blade of grass and your two thumbs. Put the blade of grass straight up and down between your two thumbs, holding your thumbs side by side. Hold your thumb instrument to your lips and blow.

Now, here is a musical instrument you can make out of your two hands. Have you ever seen an ocarina? People also call it a sweet potato, because it is shaped like one. It is a kind of hollow shell with a hole at one end to blow on. It also has several holes along the top for the fingers to play.

You can make an ocarina out of your hands like this:

Fold your hands tightly, one around the other. Make sure there are no open spaces, not between the fingers, not between the palms where they meet at the back.

Put your thumbs straight up, side by side, at the front of your folded hands. Bend the thumbs a little bit, so that there is a small opening between the knuckles.

Now put your lips tight against the top of that little opening. Blow over the opening.

It will take a little work before you get a musical sound. It comes out as a rather deep sound. It goes "Toot!"

Once you get that sound, try to make some others. Lift one finger and blow. That will make a higher sound.

Try lifting different fingers, one at a time, and see what sounds you can play on your hand ocarina.

Dancing Fingers

Now we go from musical hands to dancing fingers. Fingers can be puppets.

Your finger puppets can be any kind of people you want to make them. You can make them act out any kind of play that you make up for yourself.

Here is your first puppet—a thumb puppet. With your water paints or crayons, make a little face on the front of your thumb. Now fold one hand around the other with your thumb puppet inside. And now pop your thumb puppet up and let him make a bow.

The man who made up this puppet made it a little boy puppet. He named it Theodore Thumbpuppet.

You can give a whole show, just with your thumb!

You can make a whole family of puppets out of your two hands. You can make a clown, a ballet dancer, a four-footed animal. You can make an insect or an octopus with many wriggling legs. Of course, the insect or the octopus will have only five legs, but you can make them wriggle like six or eight!

Here's what you do:

Decide what kind of creature your finger puppet is going to be. Now draw or paint the puppet's face on the back of your hand. Two eyes and a mouth are usually enough to give the idea. For a clown, make a white face and a thick red nose.

Cut a fringe of paper of the right color for its hair. Make it into a bracelet to go around your wrist, so that the hair comes down like bangs over the forehead. (Use some Scotch tape to fasten the bracelet on the inside of your wrist.) You can draw

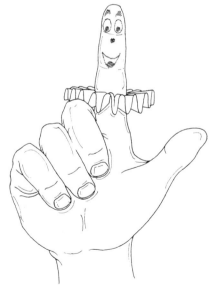

or paint a hat on top of the bangs, on the front of your wrist.

The legs of your puppet are your forefinger and your middle finger. Its arms are your thumb and your little finger. (Your ring finger is out of this, if it is a two-legged puppet. Just tuck that finger out of the way as best you can.)

Color the legs any way you like. Make them red and yellow for a clown's pants. Color them pink for a ballet dancer. Make her a little, stiff ballet skirt out of paper and stick it on with Scotch tape just at the top of her legs. If your puppet is a boy or girl, dress it in a bright pair of shorts. Put some painted or crayon-colored sleeves on your puppet's arms.

You can make little paper shoes to fit over your puppet's fingertip feet.

For a four-legged animal puppet, use all four fingers as your puppet's legs. (Your thumb is out of this. Tuck it inside your palm.)

For an insect or an octopus, use all your fingers and your thumb as well. Color them any way you like. Give the creature big eyes on the back of your hand. Make its legs wriggle.

Make your finger puppets talk with different voices. Have a pair of them, one on each hand.

Have fun with your finger puppets!

14

HANDS CAN DO MAGIC

A magician uses lots of things for his magic. He waves his wand, and coins, cards, rabbits, pitchers of water, and even people appear and disappear.

But a magician's real magic is not in the things he uses. His real magic is in his hands. His hands are so quick that his audience sees only what he wants them to see.

Here is a trick of hand magic that you may already know called the Thumb Trick.

Stretch out your left hand with the fingers flat and together and the palm facing you.

Bend your left thumb down toward your palm. Bend it from the top joint, so that only half of the thumb shows above your fingers from the front. (Do this trick in front of the mirror a few times so that you get it just right.)

Now bend your right thumb from the top knuckle. Put the knuckle of that thumb against the knuckle of the other one. Put your right forefinger over the place where your right thumb and your left thumb come together.

From the front, your two thumbs together look like one thumb.

Now, with a wrench and a groan, and a look of pain on your face, pull your right hand away with half a thumb. (But pull it only about half an inch away, so that your left hand still hides the Trick.)

Now move your right hand back, and put the two halves of your poor thumb together again.

Give a sigh of relief and show your thumb all whole and well.

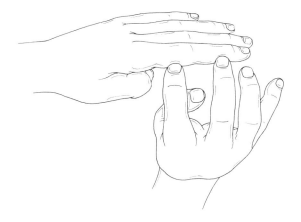

More Hand Magic

Make a snake wriggling in your hands, like this:

Hold your hands together with the palms touching, and your fingers out straight and together.

Now bend your middle fingers and cross them over, so that each finger is over the back of the other hand.

Now turn your hands, still keeping them together, so that the fingers of each hand point toward the wrist of the other hand.

Your middle fingers stick out, one on each side of your hands. Wriggle those two middle fingers. That's the snake wriggling in your hands!

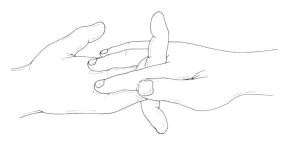

For this trick you will need a large handkerchief or a napkin. Roll the handkerchief up and take hold of one end in each hand. The trick is to tie a knot in it without letting go of the ends.

Do you know how to do it?

Simple.

Lay the rolled up handkerchief straight on the table. Fold your arms. Now pick up the ends of the handkerchief, one in each hand.

Now uncross your arms, still holding the ends, and pull the handkerchief out straight.

There it is, with a knot in it. And you did not let go of the ends to tie it.

Finger Magic

Prove to your friend that you have eleven fingers.

Count the fingers of one hand backward, like this: ten, nine, eight, seven, six. Now hold up the fingers of the other hand. How many are there? Five, of course. How much are six and five? Eleven!

Show your friends that you have only nine fingers.

When they are not looking, clasp your two hands together, putting the fingers of one hand between the fingers of the other. But leave the middle finger dangling underneath between your palms.

Now show your hands with the fingers interlaced to your friends. Ask them to count them.

Nine fingers!

Here is a way to get yourself an extra nose:

Cross your forefinger and middle finger. Now rub your nose between them above where they cross.

How many noses do you feel?

Have one of your friends cross her fingers, shut her eyes, and discover that you have two noses!

Here is a trick to get fingers all mixed up:

Cross your wrists one over the other. Turn your hands so that the palms are facing. Lace your fingers together. Now, without letting go, turn your hands over and up in front of you.

Look at your fingers, all laced together. Do you know which fingers belong to your right hand and which fingers belong to your left hand?

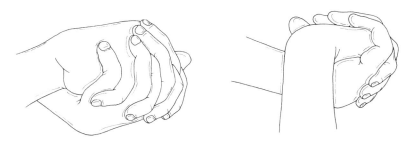

Test yourself. Try to lift the middle finger of your right hand.

Can you do it? Did you move the finger you wanted to move, the first time you tried?

If you didn't, the trick worked. It got your fingers so mixed up that they didn't know which muscles to move.

Get a friend to try the trick. When he has his hands all turned around and laced together, point to one of his fingers and ask him to move it.

(Point to the finger but don't touch it. If you touch it, the message will go to his brain that that is the finger to move, and the trick will fail. So just point.)

Probably your friend will have the same trouble you had. He will not be able to lift the right finger the first time.

You and your friend should have a good laugh over these mixed-up fingers.

Real magic takes a lot of practice. You have to be able to hide a coin or a ring in the palm of your hand and still use your hand, so that no one can guess you have something hidden there. That is called palming.

You have to be able to tuck things up your sleeve or drop them in a pocket in such a way that no one sees you do it. You have to be able to take things out of your sleeve or your pocket in such a way that nobody sees you do it.

There are wonderful magic tricks you can learn to do. Many of them are quite easy, once your hands have learned how.

So, if you like to do magic, you can begin now to practice.

Remember, the magic is in your hands.

FURTHER READING

Blumenthal, Lassor A. *The Hand Book*. New York: Doubleday, 1976.

Bursill, Henry. *Hand Shadows to Be Thrown upon the Wall*. New York: Dover, 1967.

Carlson, Bernice Wells. *Listen! and Help Tell the Story*. Nashville: Abingdon Press, 1965.

Helfman, Harry. *Strings on Your Fingers*. New York: William Morrow & Co., 1965.

————.*Tricks with Your Fingers*. New York: William Morrow & Co., 1967.

Horowitz, H. H. *Tricks Every Boy Can Do*. New York: Hart Publishing Co., 1948.

Kettlekamp, Larry. *Magic Made Easy*. New York: William Morrow & Co., 1954.

Lopshire, Robert. *It's Magic?* New York: Macmillan, 1969.

Mendoza, George. *Shadowplay*. New York: Holt, Rinehart and Winston, 1974.

Poulsson, Emilie. *Finger Plays for Nursery and Kindergarten*. New York: Lothrop, Lee and Shepard, 1921.

Van Rensselaer, Alexander. *Fun with Magic*. New York: Doubleday, 1957.